I0021597

Windows 10 in Under 90 Minutes

The Disaster To Master Step By Step User Guide

By Matt Eleck

Introduction

I want to thank you and congratulate you for downloading the book, *"Windows 10 In Under 90 Minutes: The Disaster To Master Step By Step User Guide "*

Windows 10 operating System combines the strengths of Windows 7 and those of Windows 8 to present a powerful, yet simple system designed to cater to the present and the future. Windows 8 was not received well by users due to the many changes with which desktop users were not comfortable. The lack of a Start Button was one of these issues. With Windows 10, Microsoft has strived to cater to both desktop users and tablet users.

The system has been in beta testing for a long time with a team of Windows insiders providing valuable feedback. The operating system is free for users who had genuine copies of Windows 7 and Windows 8.1 as a free upgrade. We will be looking at how you can get your copy. Those who have to buy will have to part with $119.

Windows 10 is built on what Microsoft says is a universal application architecture, making it possible for apps to run across many devices to improve the user experience. A user can access apps on the go with a phone, tablet, and PC. Microsoft has continued to say that Windows 10 will be offered as a service (unlike previous versions) and will receive regular updates that will no longer be optional to users. This is to make sure users are running a recent system and to avoid fragmentation across the platform.

The new system has received mainly positive reviews since its launch and even from its testing phase. It has been described as the best Windows OS to date. There are loads of exciting new features that improve functionality and security, as well as ensure that users have the best experience across their devices. However, there are a few issues with privacy. Some users are concerned that Microsoft is collecting a lot of personal information. We will be looking at all these and many more in this eBook.

Thanks again for downloading this book. I hope you enjoy it!

Table of Contents

Chapter 1

Preparing Your PC for Windows 10 Installation

Before installing Windows 10, you will need to take some time to prepare your PC to ensure a smooth update. There are a few things you'll need to do for this. These will include backing up your data, checking for updates on drivers, and a few others. Let us look at them in more detail.

Check out the specifications

If you are already running Windows 7 or Windows 8, then the hardware specifications will probably be adequate for Windows 10. However, just to be sure, let us look at the minimum hardware requirements for Windows 10.

You will need to have a processor with a speed of 1 GHz or faster, a RAM of 1 GB for 32 bit systems and 2 GB for 64 bit systems, disk space of at least 16 GB for 32 bit systems and 32 GB for 64 bit systems, and a DirectX 9-capable video card with a WDDM driver. If you do not want to do all of this checking and you run Windows 7 or Windows 8.1, you can just click on the Windows icon on the right hand side of your machine and select the "Check My PC" option. This will check and determine if it can run Windows 10.

You will probably need to free up some space to install Windows 10. This will be mostly in the C partition of your hard disk. There are a few options here; you can try clicking on the Disk Clean Up button which will free up some space. However, this might not be enough; if so, you could try deleting some files from this disk or uninstalling some programs that you rarely use. You will need to go to the Control Panel and select which program to uninstall in Windows 7. In Windows 8, you will go to the Start menu, go to the screen with the tiles and click on the tile you want to uninstall.

Before you install Windows 10, you might need to back up your data. In fact, this is a good practice whether you are installing a new operating system or not. There are various ways to back up data, but the best is to use the various cloud storage services available. Google Drive, Dropbox and OneDrive are some good services. If you have a Microsoft account, this will be very easy from your operating system. Windows 8 users will use the file history feature in the operating system to automatically back up files. In Windows 7, the best method is to make use of the tool that enables you to create-- a system image. This serves as a backup in case you need to roll back to your old operating system. You do so by heading to the Control Panel, and then Back Up Your Computer under User Systems and Security. Choose the Create System Image tool. It is advisable to save this image in an external drive. In case you need to roll back, this image will restore your old operating system as well as all programs and drivers that were installed. If there arises a need to go back to the old operating system, you just need go to the Control Panel, click Recover, and then Advanced Recovery Options. You will then get a prompt to select the system image you created.

The final issue I want as to look at under preparing your computer is updating your device drivers. When installing a new version of an operating system, you will need to verify if the drivers you are using are compatible. This is an issue that causes a lot of problems when switching between operating systems. We have often heard of people getting so frustrated after using a new system and experiencing some stability issues. Drivers are normally issued by your PC manufacturer. Most of these manufacturers have already made the drivers for Windows 10 available. You need to go their website and learn more. Alternatively, you could use the DXDIAG tool in Windows to check the drivers and update them.

In hardware, some devices in the old OS may not be supported in the new OS. You will get a notification about the same. Some devices may need to be uninstalled and new drivers installed during the upgrade process. You could also search for new drivers after the installation if you notice some stability issues. A report from the Upgrade Assistant will detail out these issues.

For software, some programs in the old OS may not be supported in the new OS. Other programs will need to be updates to work on the new platform. This will work in most cases. You could also look out for the newest version of that software. In this case, you could install the program, then download the new version and install again in the new OS. However, if a certain program is critical to the operation of your business or even if you rely on the program for your work as an individual, it is important first to investigate whether there are stability issues with that program on the new operating systems. Check whether the developer of that program has released a new version compatible with the new OS. If you are not satisfied that the program will work as you want it to work, do not make the migration yet. Hold on till a solution is found. You do not want to get a rude surprise and fail to do your job. Normally, it takes some time for newer versions of programs to be released that will work on new operating systems seamlessly.

Planning for a migration of an operating system is something most users overlook as time wasting, only to realize later that they could have been keener when they encounter issues after installation. Take your time and weigh your options. You would rather take one hour planning than several more hours trying to recover lost data or rolling back to your old system.

Chapter 2

How to Install Windows 10

Unlike other operating systems, Windows 10 will be available to most users as an update. If you are currently running Windows 7 or Windows 8/8.1, you will be eligible for the free update to Windows 10. This is quite surprising coming from Microsoft that they are willing to provide the OS for free. Perhaps it points to the future where software will mostly be free to users. In essence, Windows 10 will be software as a service, free to the users. The only little problem is that it is not available for free to all users, but only licensed users of the previous versions of Windows.

I hope you have prepared your PC for this update as discussed in the previous chapter; it is absolutely important to do so. The next step will be to update your current system to make sure it's completely up to date. For Windows 8, you will need to make sure you update to Windows 8.1. For Windows 7, make sure you update to Service Pack 1. If it is up to date, you should see an icon on the bottom right hand corner about getting Windows 10.

Clicking on this icon will open up Microsoft's Get Windows 10 app. You will be prompted to sign up and download the new OS. You will also be able to determine if your computer is compatible. An important point to note here is that if you do not update to the new Windows 10 within a year after the date of release, you will lose your free eligibility status, so if you want it, you cannot put it off for long. Once you sign up for the new operating system, you will wait for the download and once complete, you will get the go ahead to install it. Make sure you keep your PC on and with Internet connection. You may want to note that an operating system will consume considerable bandwidth and this may impact your Internet plan and costs.

For those users who are not running on the eligible operating systems, they will have to part with $119 for Windows 10. For instance, very early versions of Windows, such as Windows XP, are not eligible for the free update. If you have been running an unlicensed Windows operating system, you will also not be eligible for the free update. You will also need to make sure that your system specifications meet the minimum requirements for this new OS. We looked at these in the previous chapter. One thing to note is the memory; Windows 10 takes up substantial memory, more than any other operating system you may have used before. We will be talking about this and how to go about it in the next chapter.

Installing the operating system after the download is complete is actually very straightforward. However, I need to remind you to back up your data. This is important, not because any data will be lost, but with installation of a new OS, you do not want to risk it. Back up on an external hard drive or in a cloud storage service. The installation process will take between 30 minutes to one hour. It will actually depend in how fast your machine is and if you wish to customize settings at this stage. You will mostly be clicking on "next" at every step.

When you get to the configure settings step, you have the option of either choosing the express settings or customizing the settings. It is better to carry out some customizations at this stage to how you would like the system to behave. Issues such as location, browser settings, Wi-Fi connection, and others will come up. You will need to decide which settings to change. These settings heavily impact your privacy. I will dedicate a chapter to talk about privacy issues in Windows 10.

After you finish the customization, the installer will finish and will take you to the desktop. At this stage, it is important to run an update cycle to get any recent updates and to make sure the drivers are up to date.

Chapter 3

Doing a Clean Install of Windows 10

There are several reasons why you will need to do the clean install rather than go the easier way of updating your previous version of Windows to Windows 10.

The first reason might be that you are still waiting for your new OS to download to your PC. You registered and reserved a copy of the OS, but it still has yet to get to you. This is an issue that Microsoft has said is because there are so many people waiting to get the software. Delivering the new OS to all of these people takes time. However, with the clean install, you will get your version of the OS faster.

Another reason to do a clean install is that if you upgrade to Windows 10, you will be coming with all your data, programs, apps, settings from the older OS. This will definitely affect performance in the new OS, considering the fact the new system will require more resources, especially RAM. We will be looking at how to get a clean install of the Windows 10 to avoid this. When getting a clean install, you will have to back up your data. A clean install wipes out your hard drive, and thus you must have a back up if you want to continue using the files. You might need to do a clean install if you want to pass on your PC to somebody else, this will wipe out all your data in an unrecoverable form. Give the new user just a brand new OS.

Clean installation is advisable if you note that after the migration, you have been having instability issues or your system is considerably slower. Over time, your PC will store a lot of files even those you has deleted. It is good to give it a refresh once in a while.

Other times, you have purchased a PC and the manufacturer has included the OS together with some other bloatware, which might slow down your computer. You could choose to do a clean install and have only what you need.

In the case of Windows 10, we will look at two scenarios. The first is the one in which you have just updated you Windows 7 or Windows 8 but have not yet received your copy of Windows 10. There is a way to bypass the queue and get your copy. Alternatively, you might not have reserved your copy but you need this new OS. The only provision is to have genuine Windows 7 or Windows 8 installation – meaning you have a valid product key for the older version. The other scenario we will look at is that you have already installed Windows 10, but want a clean install to get rid of some issues you might be experiencing.

The only thing you need to note is that you will not be eligible for the free Windows DVD player app that is being offered to users of Windows Media Center if you do a clean install. This is not something to worry about, as you can always get the same functionality with other media players.

If you have already been running Windows 10, and you need a clean install, you will need to reset the operating system. There is a reset feature available that will turn back this OS to its fresh state. Unlike the upgrade process, you might lose all your data here, so make sure you have backed up what you need.

To reset your system in Windows 10, you will need to move to the setting app and choose update and security option. Select "Recovery" and click on the "Get Started" button, which will be under "Reset PC." Here, you will have various options.

Since we want to do a clean install, choose the second setting, which removes all of your files, settings, and programs. This will take some time to finish, as it will be wiping your disk clean. Once you do this, the files will not be recoverable. If you want to pass on your PC to somebody else or you are selling it, this is the option you should always use to make sure that your data or personal files cannot be accessed.

The other scenario is where you have not already upgraded to Windows 10. Most users will be at this point and might be confused on how to do a clean install. There is some incorrect information that Windows 10 is only available as an update on previous Windows. This is not the case; you can still get it the normal way we install operating systems. The catch here is to make sure you follow all the steps to retain your license and get the OS free.

The first thing you need to do is to update your Windows 7 or Windows 8. When you do this, and Windows confirms that you are eligible to get Windows 10, you will be good to go. What happens at this point is that Microsoft will associate your PC with a specific license key so that when you install Windows 10, you will not be asked for the product key. It activates your computer to get Windows 10 for free. Even when you install Windows 10 again in the future, you will not need the product key, as your PC will already be registered with Microsoft's servers. The OS will automatically activate itself. That is why you need to update you system first to make sure your PC is registered and eligible for Windows 10. This offer is only valid for one year from the date of launch, so you cannot postpone it forever.

Follow the upgrade process. It's simple – you just need to follow the prompts.

Once you have finished with this, you will confirm if your copy of Windows is activated before proceeding to do a clean install. You can do this by heading to settings, select "Update and Security," then select "Activation." You will see the message "Windows is activated," and you can now proceed to do a clean install. Do not do a clean install until you see this message.

To do a clean install from this point, you will need to download the Windows installation media. I know this might sound a little bit confusing, since you had already downloaded the OS through the reservation process. But you will need to download the OS in a manner that can be installed. You will head to the Microsoft website and download the Windows 10 installation files. You will have a choice either to create USB installation media or an installer DVD. For the USB installation, you will need a USB device that has at least 3 GB storage. For the DVD installation, you will need to burn the file in a DVD. You will choose what's appropriate for you. Choose the create installation media for another PC.

Select the correct installation type. Your previous version was either 32 bit or 64 bit. If you are not sure, you can still create installation media for both systems. The installer will select the right system in the installation stage.

Now the last step will be to install Windows 10 the normal way you install an operating system. You will need to connect either the USB drive or the DVD and restart your PC. Boot it from that device to start the installation.

When you get to the stage where you are asked for a product key, skip that step since you do not have the key and took advantage of the free upgrade offer. If you purchased your copy of the Windows 10, you will need to put in the key. You will go ahead with the installation until the step where you will be asked which type of installation you need. You should select the custom install option, then go ahead and do a clean install.

You will have the option either to overwrite the Windows partition (normally called disk C) or overwrite the entire hard disk to delete everything. If you overwrite everything, you will need to create new partitions.

When you finish, you will be asked for a product key once again. Skip this step. The system should activate itself after a while, but you have to be connected to the Internet. This happens when Microsoft confirms your hardware is eligible for the free upgrade since you did the registration in the earlier step. This activation may take a while if the servers are busy, so do not worry; it will eventually recognize your PC and activate it.

However, there is a way in which to force the activation if you are conversant with the command prompt. Open the administrator's command prompt, type this command, and press enter.

slmgr.vbs /ato

You can still find the activation not happening. Restart your PC and run this command again.

Chapter 4

How to Fix Common Windows 10 Installation Errors

Just like in any other software or OS release, there are bound to be a few issues here and there. Some of these issues are known, and Microsoft is working to fix them. Other issues are a result of installation errors. In this chapter, we will look at the commonly reported problems and how to fix them.

Error 0x800F0923:

You get this error when one or more drivers on your old OS are not compatible with Windows 10. This will be in the installation process. Go back to your Get Windows 10 app and click on "Check Your PC." This will identify the driver or software that has the incompatibility issues. Now go to the Microsoft's support website and check on the update to this driver or software. If there are no updates, uninstall the program or driver and continue with the installation process. You will then install this driver or program afresh after you have finished installing Windows 10.

Error 0x80073712:

This error means a file needed by Windows update is missing or damaged. The update will not install. This error has been experienced mostly by Windows 8.1 users; some Windows 7 users have also had the same problem. According to Microsoft, the issue will occur if the Component Based Servicing is corrupt. This simply means that the Windows update file has been corrupted and subsequent updates will fail to clean these damaged files. However, there is a solution to this error.

For Windows 8 or 8.1 users, you will need to use system file checker to repair the damaged Windows update files.

Open an elevated command prompt.

Run the scannow/sfc command

Then try to install the update again

If this still does not work, use the DISM tool to fix the corrupted Windows update files.

Open the elevated command prompt

.

Run the DISM.exe /Online /Cleanup-image /Restorehealth command. This command will use the Windows update to process files that will fix the corruptions. However, if your Windows update client is broken, you will need to use a different Windows installation as the repair source. You could use a different Windows PC, and use a USB drive or Windows DVD as the source of the files. To achieve this, you will run the following command:

DISM.exe /Online /Cleanup-Image /RestoreHealth/Source:C:\RepairSource\Windows /LimitAccess

C:\RepairSource\Windows is a placeholder and should be replaced with the location of your repair source.

Error 0x80200056:

This error code will mean that your PC restarted during the upgrade process. You will need to perform the upgrade again. Make sure your PC is plugged in to power throughout the process. Remember we mentioned earlier that the upgrade might be slow and take days before the OS is delivered to your PC. It will actually depend on how busy the Microsoft's servers are at that particular time. However, this problem will not last for long, as the servers deliver the OS to more people thereby, reducing the congestions.

Error 0x800F0922:

This is a common error. It simply means that your PC lost connection to Windows Update servers. Check into your Internet connection. You might switch it off then try connecting again. Make sure that you have enough bandwidth since the OS will be about 3 GB.

This error might also mean that there isn't enough space in the System Reserved partition to deliver the OS. You will need to increase the size of this partition through one of the software available for this.

Error 0xC1900208 – 0x4000C:

This error occurs when an app locks the upgrade from completing. Check out which app is causing this and first uninstall it. You will reinstall it once through installing Windows 10.

Error 0x80070070 – 0x50011, 0x80070070 – 0x50012 and 0x80070070 – 0x60000:

You might encounter this error if your PC does not have enough space on the hard drive. You will need to delete some items to create more space. You might also need to uninstall some programs if you have a lot of programs installed that are taking up all the space in the disk C.

Windows 10 activation problem

Some users are reporting getting the error message "Windows not activated." This is after performing a clean install. If you have a genuine copy of Windows 7 and Windows 8.1, the system will activate by itself. We also discussed how to force the activation through the command prompt after clean installation. However, if the OS still does not activate, there is the option of activating by phone.

Error 0xC004C003 is an activation error meaning your PC lost connection to the Microsoft activation server. When this happens, try activating again and make sure you have an Internet connection running.

Error 0xC004F061 means that you are attempting to activate Windows 10, but you did not qualify for a free upgrade. If you had a genuine version of the Windows 7 and Windows 8, you should reinstall these versions to your PC and upgrade again.

KB3081424 fails to install, stuck at 30%

This is an update to Windows 10, 64 bit systems. It was released to fix a few bugs and improve functionality. However, for some users, this update does not install and gets stuck at 30%. The following error comes up: "We couldn't complete the updates, undoing the changes." When this happens, the system reboots and undoes the changes. There is not an official fix yet, but someone has worked around this problem and provided a solution.

The problem is caused by invalid registry files. These files are located at

(HKEY_LOCAL_MACHINE / SOFTWARE / Microsoft / Windows NT / CurrentVersion / ProfileList)

Remove these files, since they are associated with a user account that no longer exists in the system after the upgrade. Remove these files and start installing the update again.

Fixing Windows 10 high memory usage

Windows 10 uses up a lot of memory that might make your PC slow down. Even when you are not running any programs, the system will still use up most of the RAM. This can be very frustrating, especially to users whose PCs have smaller amounts of RAM. The RAM usage starts normally around 130 MB, but this grows with time to over

1 GB. Even after you close down processes, the usage will be high. It is the system using up all the RAM. A restart might work for a short while before the problem comes back again.

It has been determined that faulty drivers are the cause of this problem. Follow the below procedure to fix this issue.

Install the Windows Drivers Kit.

Run the command prompt

Type cd C:Program Files (x86)Windows Kits8.1Toolsx64 and press Enter to go to the directory in the command prompt where WDK was installed

Type poolmon.exe then press Enter. Press P to sort via pooltype then B to sort it according to number of bytes

Note down the pooltag of the item which is using a majority of the memory. Open another command prompt to check which driver the tag belongs to. For this, type f indstr / s, then the tag that you have noted.

The command will point to a specific sys file. Open the file properties to check which driver the file belongs to. When you find out the driver, head over to the Microsoft site to download the official driver for Windows 10.

Fixing Wi-Fi issues in Windows 10

Some users have experienced problems with their Wi-Fi after installing Windows 10. The PC won't detect any wireless network even when your network adapter works just fine. This problem might also affect ethernet connections. Microsoft has acknowledged this issue, explained it, and provided a solution.

The issue is caused by older VPN software present in the upgrade process. The older software has a driver known as a filter driver or the Deterministic Network Enhancer which doesn't upgrade properly leading to the issue. Luckily, there is a solution to this.

Launch Command Prompt as Admin. For this, right-click Start button from there and select Command Prompt (Admin) from the drop-down menu

Execute the following command and then press Enter

reg delete HKCRCLSID{988248f3-a1ad-49bf-9170-676cbbc36ba3} /va /f

Enter the below command and press Enter

```
netcfg -v -u dni_dne
```

Now restart your PC and connect to your Wi-Fi. Another solution would be to uninstall the VPN software before the upgrade, then reinstalling it back after you are successfully upgraded to Windows 10.

Windows 10 battery issues

Microsoft and Intel have both announced that there is a bug in Windows 10 that reduces the battery life for up to 10%. Before they give us a solution, you could try saving your battery by reducing the number of services that run in the background. You could also dim the brightness on the screen to save some power.

Chapter 5

How to Roll Back to Your Previous Operating System

You might upgrade to Windows 10 and experience some challenges that will make you want to go back to your old, tried, and tested system. This is very possible and in fact, some users actually roll back as a matter of urgency since their PC might be critical to their business or day to day operations.

However, you have a time limit in which you can do this seamlessly. You can roll back 30 days after the upgrade. This time limit is meant to give you a feel of Windows 10. After this time limit, it is assumed that you have decided to continue using the new operating system. In any case, if you already used it for 30 days, you are comfortable using it. However, you could still roll back after 30 days by installing the old operating system manually. This will not save your settings or programs. After rolling back, you can still upgrade to Windows 10 any time you wish.

To roll back, move to the settings page and click on "Update and Security." Choose the recovery option and click on "Get Started." Now under Go Back to Windows X

(X is the previous version of Windows), click on "Get Started."

You will need to provide a reason why you want to roll back; just put in the reason. This will help Microsoft in determining the challenges that users face and how to solve them.

You will get a warning and a confirmation before the rollback starts. It will take some minutes to completely roll back. Anywhere between 30 minutes to one hour depending on the speed of your PC.

Once the rollback is complete, some apps may disappear and you might need to reinstall them again. Do a quick check on which programs have not rolled back. You will need to remember the logins of your previous Windows, as this is to what you will now revert. The logins you had created for Windows 10 will disappear.

Chapter 6

New Features to Look Out For

Windows 10 comes packed with so many new features that it has been dubbed the ultimate Windows operating system. When Microsoft released Windows 8, many Windows 7 users did not bother to update to the new OS, primarily because of the drastic changes with which they were uncomfortable. The new OS felt different and alien to them. The lack of a start button, which is so precious to many Windows users, felt strange. The user interface was also very different.

With Windows 10, Microsoft has tried to change the user interface and make it more familiar and reintroduced the start button. There are also many new exciting features that make the operating system much more flexible and offer much more in terms of user experience. Let us look at some of the top new features that you have to try out in Windows 10.

The User Interface

A big reason why users felt uncomfortable with Windows 8 was that they felt that they touch screen user interface was being forced on them. The interface was appropriate for a device with touch screen capabilities, making users who use the mouse and keyboard feel a bit strange.

With Windows 10, the interface has been made to look and feel modern but it has been made to work for both touch screen users and those who still prefer the mouse and keyboard.

They have introduced new ways to manage multiple Windows on the desktop for those who want to multitask (who does not?) and made it easier to window full screen apps.

Microsoft has stated that Windows 10 is built from the ground and user experience was a key consideration. Mobile and cloud computing were also key. The desktop had to be lightweight as it will run in Pcs and mobile devices. In fact, their new user interface is a step to the future where smartphones and tablets have overtaken PCs. However, it still has to be friendly to the mouse and keyboard user while at the same time being optimized for touch. The same interface will be present across the devices you use making it seamless and hassle free. The modern user is sophisticated and wants to be able to manage their devices across a single platform without wasting time maneuvering.

The Windows 8 start screen has been retained in Windows 10, though it is smaller. However, you can resize it as you wish. The live tiles will be found on the right of the desktop, which enables a user to quickly check unread emails or check the calendar. The tiles are important if users make good use of them. Rather than pinning shortcuts to apps as many people normally do, pin a shortcut to a certain function within an app that you frequently use. This will make it more convenient and faster. For instance, you could pin a certain page in a social media app or a route journey you often use in a map app.

At the bottom of the screen, beneath the app thumbnails, you will find a new bar showing virtual desktops. This is a new feature in Windows 10 that enables user to create virtual desktops on which to launch apps. In previous Windows operating system, users had to use third party programs to make use of virtual desktops but this is no more.

If you wish to flip through the desktops, you can use Ctrl+Win+left cursor or Ctrl+Win+right cursor to find what you need. This is particularly useful if you have many open windows, rather than using the normal Alt+Tab.

Just like in Windows 8, you can use the Snap Assist to snap apps to the screen. The only difference is that in Windows 10, you can snap up to four apps, each filling a quarter of the screen.

Start menu

The new start menu is part of the changes to the Windows interface but I have chosen to discuss it on its own. In Windows 8, the start menu (which is the Windows logo button that is used to navigate around their PC) was scrapped in favor of the full screen start menu. Many users did not take this well, as they were accustomed to the start button. The new feature was confusing and rather than take time to understand it, some users chose to do away with the whole system and go back to their beloved Windows 7. Part of the reason Microsoft had done away with the start button was to optimize performance for touch devices. However, in Windows 10, with the realization that users were still attached to the mouse and keyboard, they have brought back the start button.

What the new start menu has accomplished is to blend between the traditional start menu from Windows 7 – where users can still access their files and other parts of the PC from this button – but also retain the live tiles of Windows 8, where users can customize recently used apps and more specific functions within an app which they frequently use for ease of access.

The new start menu offers some surprise to those users not familiar with Windows 8. However, the fact that it offers dual functionality with the start menu and the start screen makes it friendly to all users. You even have the option to customize the menu and make it work better.

The start button launched the usual short cuts to your apps and files on the left and on the right. You will find tiles to

Windows apps such as Mail, Calendar, or even News. If you want to make some apps have some tiles shortcuts, you right click on the app and click the "Pin to Start Menu" option. If you want it to appear in the taskbar instead, right click and choose the "Pin to Taskbar" option. If you want to manage any app, right click on it and four options will be presented. Open, Uninstall, Pin to Start Menu (or Unpin if already pinned), and finally "Pin to Taskbar" (or Unpin if already pinned). You can choose to manage which apps you pin to the start menu and which to the taskbar depending on the frequency of use.

If you want to manage apps that are already appearing as tiles on the start screen, you should right click on the tile and some options are presented to you: "Unpin from Start," "Pin to Taskbar," and "Resize." You can also choose whether to turn tile live or turn live off.

All of these customizations are meant to make users have the freedom to choose how much they want to remain with the traditional start menu or by going more on the start screen. It will also depend on the device you are using. PC users will usually find the start menu friendlier, whereas tablet users will find the start screen friendlier due to the touch function.

Chapter 7

Cortana Virtual Assistant

Microsoft has offered a virtual digital assistant to enable users to quickly navigate. This is similar to Google Now and Siri, but in the context of a Windows PC, it can achieve much more. This is their intention and so far, this feature has been dubbed the stand out addition to this new operating system. Microsoft never had a digital assistant in the previous operating systems. They introduced Cortana on the Windows Phone and after finding it important to users, they have gone ahead to bring it to Windows 10.

Cortana provides useful information after a voice command, hence its effectiveness. It is built onto the native search function and pulls results from both local and web based data. You can highly customize it to your unique requirements, making it very powerful. The assistant will also constantly keep crawling your mail and calendar and provide updates on events, schedules, travel plans, and much more without even requesting it. The good thing with Cortana is that it is fully voice controlled. You can even activate it by using a "Hey Cortana" voice command, though to do this, you will have to change the default settings. Once activated, you can perform a whole range of functions with it. You can send email to your contacts, perform any search (whether in your PC or from the web), set alarms and reminders, add calendar events, and set reminders to get notifications on them. You could check the status of a certain flight, navigate through a map, and know your current location. You can launch apps and control your playlist.

There is so much you can achieve with Cortana. It opens up a new era of talking to your PC and getting results. Cortana is located besides the start button. It takes the form of a search box and any result will appear above it. You can input your search queries in the search box for both local and web based searches.

To activate the complete voice command by saying "Hey Cortana," you will have to go to the task bar and click on the search box, then click on the notebook icon on the left of the Windows and click on the setting icon. You will find a button to enable Hey Cortana. When this is activated, you will be ready to use the virtual assistant any time you need it. You can just go on the normal way you use your PC, when you need Cortana to do something, just stand the command with Hey Cortana followed by the other commands. Do not wait for Cortana to launch; it will be listening to you. It is that effective. However, if you activate this setting, Cortana will be running in the background and hence eating up some of your resources. Another thing to note here is that the Cortana service is hosted in the cloud, not on your PC, so any updates are done in the cloud, making this assistant highly effective. You do not need to run an update. New commands and functionalities are continually being added. If you have used Cortana before on the Windows phone, just use your Microsoft ID to log in and you will find that your settings will roll over to the PC.

It is not that serious when Cortana is involved. She will do all manner of silly things you might want her to do. Tired after a long day at the office? Ask for a joke from Cortana, or even make her sing a song. You can even make her joke about Siri. By this, she shows she is highly intelligent and powerful, and not only will she provide valuable information and remind you of your schedule, but she can be sarcastic and funny as well. If you would like to know, Microsoft used voice actress Jen Taylor to record the scripted dialogue that Cortana uses.

The strength of Cortana is dependent on the user and how you customize and integrate it in your day-to-day activities. For instance, by allowing Cortana to view your calendar and access your location, you will be able to get reminders on upcoming meetings and events, get traffic updates in the morning, and weather updates. You can also use Cortana to locate the nearest service providers such as restaurants or specialized shops. You can get news relevant to you based on your location or any other category of news you choose. When you check, you get three news headlines from each category you have chosen. When Cortana gets to know the location you associate with home or work, you can then set reminders such as "Remind me to call my boss when I get to work" and when you get to that location, you get the reminder.

Cortana learns your voice and will recognize it even when there are other noises coming from the background such as music or other voices. The greatest strength lies in the way you customize this function to suit your daily needs and make it more convenient for you to access files, search the web, and go about your daily life. With time and effort, you will learn about the capabilities of Cortana and to what extent you can customize her. If you needed a reason why you should upgrade to Windows 10, this is a good one.

Chapter 8

The Calendar, Photos and Mail Apps

As you would expect of any new operating system, these apps have been souped up a great deal to make them more beautiful, have more functionality, and convenient to use. They are regarded as core apps that come installed with the operating system, and Microsoft aims to have users actually make use of them without the need for third party apps.

The Mail and Calendar apps have has a new interface and new features. Actually, most of these features come from the Outlook app on iOS, which was rated highly by users. The new apps also support a variety of other email and calendar services, which is very good since you can easily set up your email, as we will be looking at shortly. These apps, especially Email and Calendar make Cortana work efficiently. Cortana will be constantly exploring them to send you reminders of upcoming events; you can even send an email through a voice command.

Calendar app

The Calendar app will now support Google Calendar. This is a new feature that was not available for Windows 8. It seems Microsoft has understood the concept of giving the users what they want. Shared Google calendars will work fine with seamless support. This new calendar app looks beautiful.

Mail app

In Windows 10, the name of the Mail app is Windows 10 Mail Client. They have abandoned the Outlook express. However, this new app is more functional. There is touch support which you can use to read and delete emails easily.

Drag and drop moves email across folders. It's a really modern mail app which you should make your default mail client.

To set your mail on Windows 10, you will just need to link your PC with your Windows account if you were a previous Outlook client. All of your settings will move over to this new app. However, if you need to set up for the first time, it will take a few minutes to set it up.

The new mail will accept all the standard mail systems. So no matter where your email address is based, (Gmail, Outlook, Yahoo, iCloud, POP IMAP) you can easily set up for this mail client. You will need to enter your email address and password. Windows mail will then set up the server settings based on your email.

You might be asking why you need a mail client. There are many reasons why viewing your mail from a mail client is better than from the web browser page. For one, you get to receive a notification in your PC at the action center of any email. You also get to manage your emails much more easily and sync email with other apps such as calendar, Cortana, and others. You could also set up multiple accounts and easily switch between them.

We have looked earlier on touch functionality. You can easily swipe from left to right to flag and email or from right to left to archive it. These are for users who have touch-enabled devices. For mouse and keyboard users, you can hover over action buttons to either archive, flag, or delete an email. You can also use the mouse to drag and drop emails to specific folders.

The mail app offers various formatting options for your email message – much more than has been seen in other email systems. This helps in drafting even the most demanding email and making sure the message gets home. When entering a contact, an autocomplete list of contacts will appear based on the first character you type and also frequently emailed contacts.

The Photos app

The Photos app is a built in app with a new interface and great new features. The modern tech user wants to take, edit, and share photos in real time, and this app enables them to do so. It connects to the OneDrive service for easier sharing and storing of photos. Images can be enhanced quickly through basic editing tools. You do not have to be an expert in photo editing; just a few quick edits to make sure the photo looks as you want it. The Photos app organizes your photos by dates and creates curated albums for you. This is very nice feature, especially for people who take a lot of photos. You can easily share these photos via the various social media platforms as well as through email.

The Photo app has two sections named Collection and Albums. In the collection section, there will be all your photos grouped by the date you took them. This comes in handy when you want to search for a certain photo, you do not have to scroll through but rather you narrow down to the time period in which you took it and search from there. The other section is the album section which will have your photos grouped together in albums. The app will curate these photos based on location, facial recognition, and date taken.

The photo app will access your photos and videos from the pictures folder on the PC and those from the OneDrive service. If you need to add a folder to this app, click on Settings, go to Sources, and click on Add this Folder to Pictures. If you do not want the app to access your photos from OneDrive, go to Settings and turn off Show My Photos from OneDrive.

Editing your photos is pretty easy. We all want to look our best before sharing our photos, hence the filters, effects, and retouch features. To edit a photo, you will open it and click on the pencil icon. On the left hand side of the photo, there will be the different editing categories, filters, basic fixes, light, color, and effects. The basic fixes option will include a one-click enhance button and others such as red-eye, rotation, straightening, retouch, and cropping. The filters and effects will allow you fix your photo the best way you know how. You can always undo and redo any changes till you get the best photo. As you do this, you will have the option to compare the edited photo to the original. You do so by clicking and holding the compare button, which will be at the top of the screen.

Chapter 9

The New Edge Browser

For many years and many versions of operating systems, Microsoft has had a browser that has rarely been used. The Internet Explorer browser has been left behind by other browsers such as Chrome, Firefox, Opera Mini, and Safari. Microsoft never really improved this browser. It was susceptible to crashes and painfully slow making users loathe it. However, this has changes with Windows 10. They have done away with Internet Explorer (not completely though) and brought in brand new browser which will be known as the Edge Browser. Internet Explorer will still be available mostly for enterprise compatibility, but for the average users, the Edge Browser will be your new friend and default browser. I guess Microsoft chose to change the name of their browser completely knowing how users detested it. No amount of convincing would make users try out Internet Explorer, even if they were to be promised vast improvements. However, it is important to note that Edge is not an improvement of Explorer but rather a completely new browser. Just like other modern browsers, it is fast, lean, and supports the modern browsing experience, which is what users want.

It was imperative that Microsoft get the browser right this time, because it will enable Windows users to have a much more seamless experience when using Windows 10. For instance, you can integrate Cortana with the Edge Browser to execute voice based browsing commands.

However, just like any other new browsers, the Edge browser will be bare boned at the start. Power users might find it inadequate due to the lack of extension support, which will take time to come up. However, for the average user, it will be a good browser that you should try out.

Edge will be available across all devices from PCs to tablets to phones. It is a new clean, tight, and responsive browser. It is also fast, and that is one feature that users want. The fact that it is bare bones makes it lightweight, so it will not consume vast resources on your PC. The main issue with Internet Explorer was that it was bloated and web pages that were not being optimized for this browser. Microsoft has said that they have worked to make sure web pages built with the other browsers such as Firefox and Chrome in mind will work out well in Edge. In my experience, this has been the case.

You will be asked, "Where to next," to start your browsing experience. The search bar can be used to enter addresses as well. Below the search bar are links to popular websites, which you can customize to web pages you regularly visit. Below these are links to customized news and information feed to quickly get in the know. You could personalize this section to provide news on politics, news articles, sports news, weather information, entertainment news, and much more. The search is powered by Bing. This is unsurprising since Bing is Microsoft's search engine. In fact, they have cheekily made it hard for you to change to another service. However, with Google being the dominant search engine, most users will feel more comfortable using it. To make Google your default search engine, move to Settings>Advanced Settings>Search in the Address Bar>Add New>Choose your favorite engine from the list (in this case Google)>Add as default

Changing to a different default search engine will not change any of the other features on this browser.

Integration with Cortana is a really nice feature of this new browser. You can be able to make searches using your voice. How cool is that? When you search any common terms and things such as weather, Cortana will come in handy; you do not have to type your search query. When typing something in the search box, Cortana will offer suggestions to autocomplete your query. Cortana will also be capable of providing answers via voice for a number of search queries. Microsoft is still building upon this capability and increasing the number of results that Cortana can directly return. A different feature in Cortana known as Cortana assist will be able to quickly scan a web page for you and return useful information such as email addresses and phone numbers. Currently, this feature works with restaurants, and Microsoft says that they will expand it to other features in the future.

Other features in the Edge browser include a Reading List feature that allows you save articles and web pages for future reading. However, the saved pages will not be available offline, which is a small letdown. The browser is also capable of stripping down ads and banners from a page to make it easier to read. It also provides easier posting of links to social media through the native sharing feature. Microsoft has built Adobe Flash Support into Edge. This makes loading websites faster.

There are a few issues however with this browser. Besides the issues I highlighted earlier of lack of plugins and extensions for power users, compatibility with Google Web Apps is still an issue. If you use Google Docs and Sheets frequently, you might not have the best experience. This is a work in progress and more support will be added to make this browser useful to all users. I cannot claim that it is at the same level with Chrome, but compared with the previous browser from Microsoft, this is really a huge step forward.

Chapter 10

Continuum Makes Switching Interfaces Easy

This is another of the new exciting features in Windows 10. When Microsoft developed Windows 8, they intended to bridge the gap between PC and mobile devices. However, PC users felt that the changes were more abrupt, and most users opted to remain with Windows 7. With Continuum, Microsoft is aiming to make it possible to switch between two modes across the devices. It allows the more tablet friendly tiles interface to remain, as well as the traditional desktop interface that PC users love.

This feature works best in devices that can be turned into a tablet or a PC. A device such as Surface 3 Pro which is easily connected to a keyboard and a mouse to make it work as a PC will benefit from this feature greatly. These devices (commonly known as 2 in 1 devices), tablets, and even Windows phones will find great use of the continuum features. Your phone can be turned into a desktop interface. The Tablet mode allows users of touch-enabled device navigate easily. Microsoft is banking on the trend that shows more and more users are going for mobile devices than the traditional PC, thus positioning their operating system to be flexible on this end without losing the PC users. Continuum was built to fix this issue with Windows 8 where desktop users were forced to use the touch interface. Continuum will enable users to have the best interface at any particular time, depending mostly on the device they are currently using and the function for which they are using the device.

Continuum will mostly work automatically and detect the device you are using. However, you can change the settings to give you more control on when to switch between the two interfaces. For instance, if you are using a PC, Continuum will detect and present the traditional mouse and keyboard interface. If you are using a touch-based device either a phone, tablet, or even a PC with this capability, Continuum will switch to the Tile interface. For 2 in 1 devices, Continuum will detect when the keyboard and mouse are attached and present the desktop interface. When they are detached, it will allow you to switch to the Touch interface.

The best thing with the Continuum feature is that not only the interface is changing to give you the best user experience. Other applications also adjust accordingly to offer the user the best way to interact with them. This is made possible through the use of the Universal Apps which have the same underlying code and are able to adapt to the mobile or desktop interface.

Continuum is built in the Windows 10 operating system and as such, there is not much setting up to do. If you install the OS into a laptop or desktop, it will always use the desktop interface. If you own a tablet or a hybrid device, the feature will sense this; you can change the setting to control how it behaves. For instance, if you have a keyboard that was attached to your tablet removed; the feature will pop up a dialog box which will ask if you want to change to the tablet mode. If you do not want this prompt, you can change in the settings and set what Continuum will always do after that action.

Go to the start menu, then go to settings, systems, and tablet mode. You will get a heading, "When my device wants to switch modes," and the following three options will appear in a drop down menu

- Never prompt me and always remain in current mode
- Always prompt me to confirm
- Never prompt me and always switch modes

Choose what is convenient for you.

If you want to switch back to the desktop mode without connecting the keyboard, you will tap the tablet mode option at the notification center and choose switch.

Another great feature of Continuum is the ability to turn your phone into a PC. When you connect an external monitor, keyboard, and mouse, you essentially turn your Windows phone into a PC. This new feature is bound to be very exciting. You can access all Microsoft apps such as Office and Outlook. You can type in a document, read a document, reply to email, and much more. You can even run two things independently on the phone's screen and on the monitor so that if you have somebody doing something on the phone such as answering a call and another doing something on the external display such as replying to emails. However, to use this feature, you must have a new version of Windows Phone, which will have the Windows 10 OS and Qualcomm chips, which enables these advanced features. As of writing this book, they are yet to be released to the market, but this function was demonstrated by Microsoft and worked fine.

Chapter 11

The New Action Center

The action center was formerly a notification panel, but with Windows 10, its serves much more. The ability to highly customize the action center and access commonly used settings are just a few of the capabilities of this all important tool. The new action center, unlike the previous predecessors, stores up notifications for you when you need to view them. Previously, a notification used to pop up and disappear. If you were not on your PC, you would have to view the individual applications one by one to find if there is something new. Of course, you decide which apps should store notifications for later review.

To display the action center on Windows 10, you will swipe from the right hand side of the screen for touch-based interfaces or tap an icon for mouse and keyboard devices. The icon is found on the right hand side of the taskbar. You could also use the desktop shortcut Windows key + A to launch the Action Center.

To enable or disable notifications

Notifications are the real reasons we have an Action Center. Any other function is peripheral. However, you get to receive important updates and notifications regarding both the operating system and the installed apps through it. You could also receive many notifications – some of which

are not welcome – from installed apps. You should therefore determine which apps should push notifications to the action center and which ones should not. Before you are able to toggle notifications on or off, you will actually have to receive at least one notification from the said app. For instance, the Facebook app has to send you a notification; maybe you received an inbox message, before you decide to turn future notification from this app off. You can turn it on at any time you wish. To turn notification on or off, you will first need to launch the Action Center, click All Settings, select System at the top left corner, then click Notifications and Actions. Toggle the switches on or off depending on which apps you want to get notifications from. You could even choose to turn off notifications at certain periods, maybe when making a presentation; you

don't want notifications to pop up on the screen. We will look at how to do this shortly.

You can also dismiss a notification without turning off future notifications from an app by mousing over the specific notification and clicking an X on the right side of the notification. This action will not launch that app. You can clear a bunch of notifications by clicking on Clear All in the upper right hand corner to dismiss all notifications.

Notification you dismiss from one device will be dismissed across all your Windows devices since this is a "Windows Everywhere App." In any case, you do not want to find a notification on something you already read or dismissed on your other device. In fact, across Windows 10, this will be a common feature. Microsoft wants to make users work across all their devices seamlessly.

Notification type

You can set up to receive as sound as well as a pop up on the right bottom corner upon receipt of a notification. If the sound is annoying, you can switch it off and allow just the pop up. The action center icon on the taskbar will blink till you read the notification. You will be able to set which notifications will still play sound even when Windows is locked, such as alarms and reminders.

The Action Center will also enable you access some of the most commonly used settings and features through this icon. These are known as Quick Actions. It is comprised of four buttons, which enables you to complete some actions quickly without needing to go to the settings page. These four buttons enable you to toggle between tablet and PC mode, quickly access the display settings, turn your Wi-Fi on or off, and access tools for location-based settings. You can change these buttons with any others you want.

Action Center>All Settings>System>Notifications and Actions, then select which settings button you want.

The Action Center has a feature known as Connect that allows users to play video and audio from the computer, but play the sound through another device through Bluetooth, WiGig, or Miracast. This is a good feature as it makes it easy to makes use of sound devices without having to wire them up with your PC.

Chapter 12

Xbox Streaming to PC

Windows 10 comes with an app that lets you stream games from your console to your PC. This is really good news for gamers. It makes use of the Windows native support for the Xbox controller and even offers the ability to record a game on your PC's drive. You will also be able to share clips of your game with your friends or fellow gamers. The best thing of this is that if you want to capture some nice action, you do not have to prerecord; when you choose to save a clip, it will capture the last 30 seconds of action prior. You will also be able to chat over voice and text across Windows platforms. Users will keep track of friends by gamertag across the different devices.

This feature is exciting as it enables gamers to use the PC rather than the TV set for their gaming. If you live in a house with other people (spouse, children, or roommates), you will no longer have to fight for the TV. This new functionality will come as a big boost to Xbox as it fights with Sony's PS4 for the gaming market.

For those who might not understand what streaming is, it is the ability of the Xbox games console to play games remotely on your Windows 10 PC. The home network will enable this either through an ethernet cable or through wireless connection. For instance, the games console could be in the living room, but you will be able to play the game anywhere, provided you can access your home network. The games console manages the game while your PC enables you to be located anywhere.

For a gamer to enable this feature, they must have a Windows 10 PC and an Xbox console. Go to settings on the console and enable streaming. Go to your Windows 10 PC, launch the Xbox app, and sign in with the same gamertag as the console. Connect both the Xbox console and the Windows PC to the home network. Ethernet connections (wired) provide a better streaming experience than wireless connections. Nevertheless, the wireless connections will still work. It is important to note that it might not be practical to access your home network adapter with an ethernet cable from all rooms. You can go around this problem by having a Powerline Network adapter, which uses the electrical connection in your home as a high-speed wired network. MoCA adapters enable the use of the existing coaxial cabling as a high-speed wired network, too.

You will need to connect your PC to the Xbox console and establish a connection. This should happen if you have already launched the Xbox app on the PC. On the PC, launch the Xbox app, click on connect on the left side of the panel. The app will start finding any connected consoles from your home network. If more than one console is connected, select the name of the console to which you want to connect. At this point, it is important to note that all consoles are normally pre-named "MyXboxOne." If you will be connecting multiple consoles, you need to rename each console to determine to which one you are connecting.

Go to Settings on the console, select System, and you will find Console name as the first option on this screen.

Once a connection has been established with the console from the app, you will see an icon change indicating this. You will also find new options for streaming, media remotes, and power. You will now have gained remote control over your Xbox console. You can launch a game either from the console or from the PC. From the console, click stream and play from the PC. From the Xbox app, click on any Xbox game in the app and start streaming. Click play from the console, which will be found on the upper right corner of the screen. The game will be launched on the console and streaming on your PC will immediately start.

You can change streaming quality any time before or during a game. Video quality will mostly be dependent on the type of connection you have. You should select the video quality that gives you a better gaming experience based on the capabilities of that type of connection. Let us look at the recommended settings. You should change the setting through the Xbox app. Click Settings>Game Streaming.

If both the Xbox One and the PC are connected to the home network through an ethernet connection, choose high streaming quality. You can also choose high quality if the console and PC are in the same room as the network router. Make sure there is minimal wireless interference. Choose medium streaming quality for wireless connections with 5 GHz wireless network for PCs and consoles in different rooms. Choose low quality for 2.4 GHz wireless networks as well as low end PCs and tablets.

To determine at which setting you experience the best gaming streaming quality, start with a high setting and reduce till you get to the best performance based on the different scenarios.

To make use of a headset for playback and recording, plug in your USB headset into the Windows PC or the controller before you begin streaming a game. Then make the headset the default audio device by opening Control Panel>Hardware and Sound>Manage Audio Devices.

There has been mixed reviews on the gaming experience while streaming on your PC. However, it has mostly been positive. The convenience that this offers to Xbox lovers is great. Another great thing is that it has enable users to make use of the old X360 pads on Xbox One, so as long as the X360 pads can connect to the PC and you are streaming the game, it will work just fine. This will be quite important for multiplayer games.

Chapter 13

Windows Hello

This is another new feature in Windows 10. Windows Hello enables users to log in to their PC without needing to type in a password. Its offers convenience and enhanced security. It is something similar to the image recognition systems that are available, but more enhanced to beat the fraudsters who normally get around such systems. To this end, Windows Hello requires special cameras that most devices on the market currently do not have. However, with the roll out of Windows 10, this is surely set to change. Just as the facial recognition technology is continually being adopted in many other areas such as banking, security, and modern cars, the tech world is catching up. The new Hello feature is something that promises to make it more popular with Windows Users, especially considering the convenience it offers. Microsoft is also confirming that they are working to spread it across other apps as well as certain web pages. We can expect more laptop manufacturers to include the special camera in their production and make this a selling point.

The working behind Windows Hello is very simple. You just sit behind your laptop as you normally do and you are logged in. Hello uses the RealSense depth camera by Intel to recognize your facial characters. The camera has three lenses; the conventional webcam is in the middle, and the right hand camera is an infrared camera that uses infrared light bouncing off from your face to recognize you.

You will have to train Hello to recognize your face at first. You can do this by moving to Settings, then Accounts, then Sign-In options, then Windows Hello.

Here you will be required to provide a four-digit PIN before starting in the Hello Authentication process. You are used to passwords on Windows, but here, you will need a PIN. Do not forget this PIN.

You will see the depth the camera sees and if your face is out of the shot, you will need to either lean your face or adjust the laptop's screen. If you wear glasses, you choose whether to have Hello recognize you with them or without them. I would suggest you have them on if you usually wear them all the time. Hello will let you know once it has recognized you. You can test it by logging off your PC and try logging in. You will just need to seat behind your PC normally. Once you have logged out, there will be an animated eye on the lock screen which will be looking out for you. Once it finds you and authenticates your face, it logs you in and winks at you. The camera switches off at this point. You do not have to be worried that it keeps looking at you.

The logic behind Windows Hello is that a user is unique in their own way. Your face, iris, and fingerprints are unique. A combination of characters to form passwords is not unique and has been known to be hacked. Using your unique biometric details to access your devices, apps, and other online content is more secure and provides a more personal experience. Users normally store their passwords within their devices or in the cloud where they can easily be accessed by malicious people. Passwords can also be forgotten especially now that we have to log in to multiple accounts on a daily basis. Making use of your biometric details is far more convenient. To make sure that your biometric details, especially the face and iris are accurately taken, Microsoft is making use of special hardware, The RealSense depth camera and special software to accomplish this. No impersonation will work; neither will tricks such as holding an image to the camera. The camera uses infrared technology to sense depth and recognize your face in various lighting environments.

Users might be concerned with security and privacy while the Hello technology. Microsoft has adhered to requirements and regulations that govern collection of biometric details. Your facial details are not stored anywhere, but rather they are encrypted. This technology is enterprise grade and will find application across security, defense, health education, and financial organizations.

Currently, there are not many laptops that have this special camera. If you are looking for a laptop with the RealSense Depth Camera in the US, look out for the following: Lenovo ThinkPad Yoga 15, Acer Aspire V 17 Nitro, Lenovo ThinkPad E550, Asus N551JQ, HP Sprout, Lenovo B5030, Asus ROG G771JM, HP Envy 15t Touch, Asus X751LD, Dell Inspiron 15 5548, Dell Inspiron 23 7000

However, if you really want to use the Hello feature, you can buy the RealSense 3D camera Kit for Intel for $100. However, this is a developer kit. At the time of writing this book, there are no webcam kits for the average users, but I bet it will not be long before Intel or another company has them on the market.

Chapter 14

Windows 10 Shortcuts

You can never claim to fully understand an operating system if you do not have a few shortcuts to common functions you use on a day-to-day basis. Windows shortcuts are combinations of characters (two or more) that accomplish a task that would otherwise require a mouse or touchpad. These shortcuts save a lot of time and enable you to quickly accomplish what you wanted to do besides showing your mastery of the operating system. Who does not want to amaze a few people by just using the keyboard to start and finish a task?

Some apps will come with some accelerator keys, which enables users to work with them easily. Check out your apps for these and how to use them run your commands. Most times in a menu, if a letter is underlined, this means that you can press the Alt key and the letter to accomplish the task rather than clicking on the menu item.

You can also customize and create keyboard shortcuts for your apps. To do so follow the following steps:

- Open the Start menu and move to All apps

- Find the app for which you wish to create a keyboard shortcut. Right click it and click the option "Open File Location." Click this and move to the next step. If you do not find the option "Open File Location," this will mean it is a native Windows 10 app or an app from the Windows store.
- If it is a native Windows app, click it and drag it from the star menu to the desktop. This creates a desktop shortcut which you will then right click and click on properties
- In the properties window that opens, click on shortcut and then find a line that says shortcut key. Type your desired shortcut keys and click apply. You will have created a shortcut key for that app.

Let us look at some useful shortcuts in Windows 10. (These are not the only ones; there are many more which you could take time to learn. Even the old shortcuts still work as well.)

Winkey 10 shortcut	Description
Winkey + Tab	Activates Task View
Winkey + A	Activates Action Center
Winkey + C	Activates Cortana with speech
Winkey + D	Shows desktop
Winkey + E	Opens File Explorer
Winkey + G	Activates the new Xbox game bar to let you record games or take screenshots.
Winkey + H	Activates share feature in Windows 10 apps
Winkey + I	Opens Windows 10 settings
Winkey + K	Activates Connect feature to stream to wireless displays and audio devices
Winkey + L	Locks a machine
Winkey + P	Project a screen
Winkey + R	Run a command
Winkey + S	Activates Cortana
Winkey + X	Opens power user features
Winkey + Left / Right / Up / Down	Snaps apps to the side of a screen (press Up or Down after snapping left / right to enable four apps to

	snap)
Winkey + Ctrl + D	Creates a new virtual desktop
Winkey + Ctrl + F4	Close virtual desktop
Winkey + Ctrl + Left or Right	Switch between virtual desktops
Winkey + Shift + Left or Right	Move apps from one monitor to another
Winkey + 1 / 2 / 3...	Open programs that are pinned on the taskbar. The first app is number one.

Chapter 15

Windows 10 Privacy Issues

Since the launch of Windows 10, there has been some discontent regarding collection of data by Microsoft. It is a hard time for them since users want a context based operating system that integrates into their lives, but at the same time, they do not want any of their data to be collected. I agree we all crave some privacy and the big corporations need to respect this fact. However, we also need our everyday computing experience to be made simpler and more personal. We therefore have to concede some information about us.

The main reason why corporations, Microsoft included, want to collect our data is to tap in to the lucrative advertising business. With more personalized data, they are able to target ads to us, which can easily convert to sales. This makes it easier for them to provide services that better suit us. However, users are wary of this as they do not know how else their data may be used or who else might have access to this data. Microsoft's privacy policy is very ambiguous. It states that they will collect information about everything you do with your Windows PC as well as your activity online. "Finally, we will access, disclose and preserve personal data, including your content (such as the content of your emails, other private communications or files in private folders), when we have a good faith belief that doing so is necessary."

Let us look at how Windows 10 upgrade will impact your privacy and where you can restrict what Windows collects.

During installation, Windows will encourage you to accept "express install," and it will seem as if it is a fast and convenient way to install your OS. However, this will make your OS share the maximum information it can about you. All your activity with the PC and online, settings, preferences, locations, contacts, events you attend, and any other information Microsoft may require. Do not accept express install; rather, go for the custom install option. This will bring in the first screen that will mostly concern location and personalization. Turn all of these off. These settings will collect your data and send it to Microsoft without any help to you. The adverting ID is not something to look forward to; I have heard some people arguing that it will help Microsoft and partners give you targeted ads that you might find useful, but I tend to disagree. In case you need anything, you can always look out for it. You do not need advertisers to tell you what you need.

The second screen will also do little to help your user experience. You can go through the options one by one, but I suggest you turn everything off here, too.

On this second screen, the first two options about smartscreen and page prediction are ways in which Microsoft wants to get more information about you. There is an option of automatic connection to your contact networks and open hotspots. Turn this off, as you cannot trust the system to accurately determine which network is good for you. Let you choose which network you want to connect to at any time. Sending error messages is not helpful to you. Microsoft might need to know what caused it as they look to fix issues, but sending the error report might send over personal information from your PC as well.

When the system has installed, move to Start Menu, Settings, Privacy, and then the Feedback and Diagnostics section. Set diagnostic and data usage to basic.

Cortana

Cortana will collect a lot of information about you. It will collect voice input, analyze speech data, it will collect information of calendar events, contacts, appointments and much more. To be fair to Microsoft, Cortana would not work as well as it does without this information. So if you are wary of this information being collected, simply do not use Cortana. If you have no problem about it, well and good, makes use of this amazing digital assistant.

Data syncing

Microsoft will sync your data and settings automatically when you sign up using your Microsoft account. This information will be stored in the company's servers. Some of the information will include browser information such as history, favorites, and open pages.

Wi-Fi sense

Wi-Fi sense is one of the features that raised a lot of concern initially. This feature enables users to share their Wi-Fi with their contacts across the different platforms without requiring them to log in using a password. This means that contact that might be in your Facebook, Skype, and Outlook apps will just access your Wi-Fi if there are close to it. This is meant to increase security, as you do not have to share your password with anybody. Your friends cannot share the Wi-Fi since they do not have any password; they can only use it. You do not have to change your password every so often. You will have to enable this feature for every network to which you connect. This feature was blown out of proportion initially, but I guess most people did not understand the concept behind it. It does not expose your private information in any way.

We cannot possibly look at all scenarios where Microsoft wants to take your information. However, whenever you encounter a situation requesting permission to collect information, always be little bit cynical, weigh your options, and determine what you are giving out Vis a Vis what you are getting. Generally speaking, avoid instances when you give out lots of personal information – not because you have anything to hide, but because you should be concerned how this information is used and what potential damage it might cause if it gets into the hands of the wrong people.

Conclusion

Windows 10 is not a finished product as of yet. Even though it has been released to the market, we can expect regular updates to follow to fix some bugs here and there and add functionality and support to the new features as we would expect of any new operating system. Update to the OS will no longer be optional. There is no button to turn off updates. This will make sure that Microsoft rolls out an update to all devices at roughly the same time. It is a step in the right direction, since important updates such as those that provide enhanced security or those that provide fixes to bugs are not left at the discretion of the user. Is common to hear a user complaining about a certain bug, yet they turned off an update that would have fixed it. Some users will even leave their system vulnerable to attacks by not updating important security patches. This will no longer be the case for Windows 10. However, you can choose when the PC will restart after the update. You do not want to lose any unsaved work caused by an unexpected update.

Windows 10 is a great operating system. There are loads of new features which show Microsoft went out of their way to deliver an operating system that would be accepted by users across the board. It seems they learned after the lukewarm reception of Windows 8 where most users chose to remain with Windows 7. The upgrade comes free for Windows 7 and Windows 8 users, so there is no reason why you should not upgrade. Make sure you try out all these cool features. If you have a tablet or Windows phone, you will enjoy the tight integration on all your devices. You can set up reminders on one or more calendar events and pick them on the other.

Thank you again for downloading this book!

I hope this book was able to help you with Windows 10!

Finally, if you enjoyed this book and it was able to help you, please take the time to help me by sharing your thoughts and posting a review on Amazon. It would be greatly appreciated!

Thank you and good luck!